CIVILIZATIONS OF THE ANCIENT WORLD

ANCIENT
PERSIA

A MyReportLinks.com Book

NEIL D. BRAMWELL

MyReportLinks.com Books
an imprint of
 Enslow Publishers, Inc.
Box 398, 40 Industrial Road
Berkeley Heights, NJ 07922
USA

MyReportLinks.com Books, an imprint of Enslow Publishers, Inc. MyReportLinks®
is a registered trademark of Enslow Publishers, Inc.

Library of Congress Cataloging-in-Publication Data

Bramwell, Neil D., 1932–
   Ancient Persia / Neil Bramwell.
     v. cm. — (Civilizations of the ancient world)
     Contents: The empire of Cyrus the Great— The land of ancient Persia — The history of the Persian
Empire— Language and religion — The people of ancient Persia— Arts and cultural contributions — The
government of ancient Persia.
   ISBN 0-7660-5251-6
1. Achaemenid dynasty, 559–330 B.C.— Juvenile literature. 2. Iran—History—To
  640—Juvenile literature. [1.Iran—History—To 640.] I. Title. II. Series.

   DS281.B73 2004
   935'.05—dc22

                              2003019334

Printed in the United States of America

10 9 8 7 6 5 4 3 2 1

To Our Readers:
Through the purchase of this book, you and your library gain access to the Report Links that specifically back
up this book.
The Publisher will provide access to the Report Links that back up this book and will keep these Report Links
up to date on **www.myreportlinks.com** for three years from the book's first publication date.
We have done our best to make sure all Internet addresses in this book were active and appropriate when we
went to press. However, the author and the Publisher have no control over, and assume no liability for, the
material available on those Internet sites or on other Web sites they may link to.
The usage of the MyReportLinks.com Books Web site is subject to the terms and conditions stated on the
Usage Policy Statement on **www.myreportlinks.com**.
A password may be required to access the Report Links that back up this book. The password is found on the
bottom of page 4 of this book.
Any comments or suggestions can be sent by e-mail to comments@myreportlinks.com or to the address on
the back cover.

Photo Credits: © 2004 Corbis Corporation, p. 1; © Corel Corporation, pp. 35, 38, 42; Art-arena.com,
p. 29; British Museum, p. 11; Clipart.com, pp. 3, 9, 13, 15, 16, 24, 28, 32; Enslow Publishers, Inc., p. 22;
Iran Chamber Society, pp. 18, 25, 31; Livius, p. 20; MyReportLinks.com Books, pp. 4, back cover;
Ozemail.com, p. 44; Photos.com, p. 39; World History, pp. 14, 26.

Cover Photo: Palace guard statue, Persepolis, and winged lion rhyton, © 2004 Corbis Corporation; Palace
ruins, Persepolis, © Corel Corporation.

Contents

ANCIENT PERSIA

MyReportLinks.com Books
Great Books, Great Links, Great for Research!

The Report Links listed on the following four pages can save you hours of research time by **instantly** bringing you to the best Web sites relating to your report topic.

How to Use MyReportLinks.com

1 Got a Report to do?

2 Check out a MyReportLinks.com Book at the Library.

3 Read the Book.

4 Go to www.myreportlinks.com for Quick, Safe, and Up-to-Date Links!

5 Internet Report Links = Great Information.

6 Write Your Report. Impress Your Teacher.

MAX LYNX

The pre-evaluated Web sites are your links to source documents, photographs, illustrations, and maps. They also provide links to dozens—even hundreds—of Web sites about your report subject.

MyReportLinks.com Books and the MyReportLinks.com Web site save you time and make report writing easier than ever!

Please see "To Our Readers" on the copyright page for important information about this book, the MyReportLinks.com Web site, and the Report Links that back up this book. Please enter **VPE8293** if asked for a password.

Report Links

The Internet sites described below can be accessed at
http://www.myreportlinks.com

▶**Persia or Iran: A Brief History**   *EDITOR'S CHOICE

Iran is the modern nation that was once the seat of the Persian Empire.
Here, you can explore this country's history from the year 3500 B.C.
to modern times. The site also contains links to other helpful sources.

▶**Achaemenid Persia**   *EDITOR'S CHOICE

This Web site contains a wide array of information on the Achaemenid
Empire of ancient Persia. Click on the red headings to learn about
different topics, from general facts about the empire to the battles
the Persians fought in.

▶**Battle of Marathon**   *EDITOR'S CHOICE

The Battle of Marathon was the first major battle of the Persian Wars,
and it was also a major defeat for the Persian army. This site offers a
history of the battle in which Darius I led his troops into Greece.

▶**Time Line of Iranian History**   *EDITOR'S CHOICE

This time line covers the history of Persia, or Iran, from 8000 B.C.
through all of the major eras in Persian history.

▶**Cyrus the Great**   *EDITOR'S CHOICE

The Persian Empire's first Achaemenid king was Cyrus the Great.
The king and ancient Persia under his rule are covered in this site,
which also contains information on the Persian Army and offers links
to other Web sites.

▶**Portland State's Greek Civilization for Kids**   *EDITOR'S CHOICE

This comprehensive Web site designed for kids has lots of information
on ancient Persia, such as its rulers, army, and laws, as well as links to
other related topics.

Report Links

The Internet sites described below can be accessed at http://www.myreportlinks.com

▶ **Achaemenid Empire**

This Web site provides a look at the Achaemenid Empire, which began with the reign of Cyrus the Great.

▶ **Alexander the Great: Overview of Articles**

In 331 B.C., Alexander the Great and his army brought an end to the Persian Empire at the Battle of Gaugamela. At this site, learn about his role in the defeat of Persia as well as his life and further conquests.

▶ **Aramaic, Language and Linguistics**

The primary language spoken by the ancient Persians was Aramaic. This site examines the origins and evolution of this language.

▶ **Architecture Before Islam**

Many architectural advancements were made during and after the reign of the Achaemenid dynasty in ancient Persia. Learn about Persian architecture and view some of Persia's most magnificent architectural achievements at this Web site.

▶ **Battle of Salamis**

After the Persian victory at Thermopylae, the Greeks and Persians met at a naval battle at Salamis. At this Web site, learn about Xerxes and the Persian Army's defeat at Salamis.

▶ **The Behistun Inscription**

The Behistun Inscription is a cuneiform text in three ancient languages that was carved into the face of a mountainous rock in what is now western Iran. A stone relief of Darius I is next to the inscription. This site examines the text and the sculpture.

▶ **Cyrus Cylinder**

This site from the British Museum contains information and an image of the Cyrus Cylinder. This cylinder is inscribed with a history of the ancestry and deeds of Cyrus the Great following his capture of Babylonia.

▶ **Darius I**

Darius I was an Achaemenid king from the years 521 to 486 B.C. This site offers a brief biography of Darius.

Report Links

The Internet sites described below can be accessed at http://www.myreportlinks.com

▶**The Empire of Cyrus II**

This site offers a look at Ancient Persia at the beginning of Cyrus the Great's rule in 529 B.C.

▶**The First Declaration of Human Rights**

When Cyrus the Great entered the city of Babylon, he made a declaration that spoke of human rights. This was inscribed on what is now called the Cyrus Cylinder. This site contains a passage about the declaration as well as a translation of part of the inscription on the cylinder.

▶**History of Iran: Median Empire**

The Medes were a group of people living near the same area as the ancient Persians for many years, before Cyrus the Great gained power. Learn about their history at this Web site.

▶**History of Iran: Pasargadae**

Built by Cyrus the Great, Pasargadae is the oldest Achaemenid capital city. Find out about this city's history and view vivid pictures at this site.

▶**King Darius III**

This site offers an account of King Darius III, the last ruler of the great Persian Empire. In 331 B.C., the Persians lost the battle of Gaugamela to Alexander the Great and his troops.

▶**Maps of the Empire**

On this Web site, you can view two maps from ancient Persia. One is from the reign of Darius I, c.500 B.C., and the other is from 343 B.C. during the reign of Artaxerxes III.

▶**Persepolis and Ancient Iran**

The great city of Persepolis, commissioned under Darius I, was the jewel of the Persian Empire. This University of Chicago site contains an extensive archive of photographs of the city's ruins as well as a brief overview of the city's history.

▶**Persia**

This Web site from the History Channel provides a brief overview of ancient Persian dynasties, from the Achaemenid Empire to the Sassanid Empire.

Report Links

The Internet sites described below can be accessed at
http://www.myreportlinks.com

▶**The Persian Wars: Greece's Finest Hours**

The Persian Wars arose from conflict between the Greek city-states and the Persian Empire and lasted for over twenty years. This Web site takes a look at the wars between Persia and Greece.

▶**Persian Wars Time Line**

The Persian Wars marked a turning point in both Persian and Greek history. This site offers a time line of the battles and includes battle descriptions and maps.

▶**Persians—History for Kids**

This site offers a brief lesson on the history of ancient Persia, including its kings and battles fought with Greece.

▶**Philip of Macedon**

From 359 to 336 B.C., Macedonia was ruled by Philip II, who dreamed of conquering the Persian Empire. This site offers an account of his life and his battles with Persia.

▶**Themistocles**

Themistocles was a commander who led Greece to victory over the Persians at the Battle of Salamis. He is known for his role in strengthening the Athenian Navy. Read about his life and contributions to the Greek military in this article.

▶**The Library of Congress—Iran**

This Library of Congress country study of Iran includes a comprehensive history of ancient Persia, the name given to Iran by the Greeks.

▶**Women's Lives in Ancient Persia**

On this Web site, you can read an article about the treatment of women and their roles in society during the Achaemenid Empire.

▶**Xerxes: King of Persia from 485 to 465**

King Xerxes ruled the Persian Empire from 485 to 465 B.C. Read about his life and time as king at this site, which includes links to other resources.

Time Line

c.3000 B.C.	Elamites are first to settle lands of ancient Persia.
c.1500 B.C.	Medes and Persians, nomadic tribes, move into Persia.
c.700 B.C.	Medes create first state in Persian plateau.
c.550 B.C.	Achaemenid Empire: Persians under Cyrus the Great overthrow the Medes.
c.545 B.C.	Cyrus extends the Persian Empire by seizing Lydia and gradually gains Greek colonies in Ionia.
539 B.C.	Cyrus captures Babylon and frees Jews in captivity there.
529 B.C.	Cyrus dies and is succeeded by his son, Cambyses.
525 B.C.	Egypt becomes part of the Persian Empire.
522 B.C.	Darius I becomes king of Persian Empire and reorganizes the government in system of satrapies.
500 B.C.–449 B.C.	Persian Wars between Persian Empire and Greek city-states.
479 B.C.–331 B.C.	Persian Empire declines.
331 B.C.	Alexander the Great defeats a large Persian Army at Battle of Gaugamela, bringing an end to the Achaemenid Empire.
c.313 B.C.–250 B.C.	Seleucid dynasty rules Persia following death of Alexander; Greek culture spreads throughout western and central Asia.
250 B.C.–A.D. 224	Parthian Empire controls Persia.
224–mid-600s	Sassanid dynasty rules Persia until the rise of Islam.

△ Archers of the Persian guard, from a glazed frieze at King Darius' palace at Susa.

Chapter 1

THE EMPIRE OF CYRUS THE GREAT

In the sixth century B.C., the land that is today the nation of Iran was the center of the largest empire in the ancient world. The kings of Ancient Persia (from *Persis,* the Greeks' name for Persia) were the leaders of a great civilization that made important advances in government, laws, and communications. The Persian Empire founded by Cyrus the Great in 550 B.C. would, within only fifty years, occupy much of the known world at the time.

▶ The Aryans and Medes

The earliest people in what is now Iran were the Elamites, who may have settled the region as early as 3000 B.C. Aryans, nomadic people from central Asia, began migrating to Iran in the 1500s B.C. After a time, there were two major groups of Aryans: the Medes in the northwest, who established a kingdom called Media, and the Persians in southern Iran. Both groups referred to their home as Iran, which translates as "land of the Aryans." By the 600s B.C. the Medes ruled the Persians. But their rule came to an end between 559 B.C. and 549 B.C., when a Persian who would come to be known as Cyrus the Great overthrew Astyages, king of the Medes.

▶ The Achaemenid Empire of Cyrus the Great

According to the Greek historian Herodotus, Cyrus was the son of an Iranian nobleman and a Median princess, daughter of the Median king Astyages. Many historians

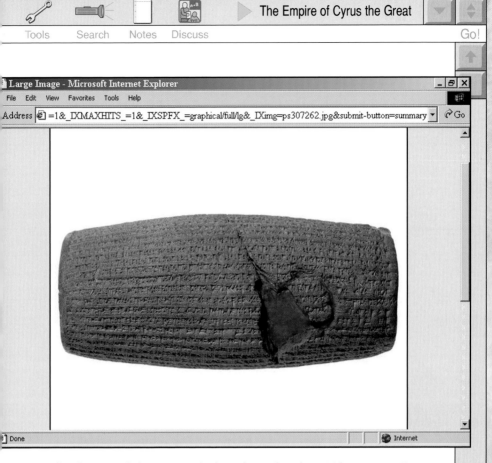

▲ This part of the Cyrus Cylinder is housed in the British Museum. Its cuneiform inscriptions declares Cyrus' intention to rule his conquered people with fairness.

dispute this account of Cyrus' background, but what cannot be disputed is that his dynasty, the Achaemenids, would rule the vast Persian Empire for more than two hundred fifty years.

Cyrus began to build his empire after the model of the great Assyrian Empire that had flourished centuries before on the banks of the Tigris River, in what is now Iraq. By 545 B.C., Cyrus had seized the kingdom of Lydia, and he gradually took over the Greek colonies in Ionia, in western Asia Minor, a peninsula in western Asia between the

Black Sea and the Mediterranean Sea that is now the Asian part of Turkey. By 539 B.C., Cyrus' armies had conquered Babylonia, and Cyrus freed the Jews who were in captivity there, allowing them to return to Palestine, which was also under his control. Although he did not conquer Egypt, he prepared the way for his son, Cambyses II, to accomplish that, in 525 B.C.

▷ A Benevolent Ruler

Cyrus' rule came to an end in 530 B.C. with his death. The empire he began would not reach its peak until the reign of Darius I, in 500 B.C., when it would encompass a region nearly as large as the modern continental United States. But Cyrus the Great continues to be admired among ancient world leaders for more than his military conquests and the empire he began.

What set Cyrus the Great apart from the rulers of most other ancient dynasties was his attitude toward the different ethnic and religious groups that existed within his empire. He had conquered many lands, and the people within those lands spoke different languages, prayed to different gods, and lived according to different customs. His tolerance and respect for the diverse cultures, customs, and beliefs of his people has led most historians to consider Cyrus a liberator rather than a conqueror.

Cyrus is also credited with being the author of what is often referred to as the first charter of human rights. The Cyrus Cylinder is an account of Cyrus' Babylonian conquest, written in cuneiform inscription on a clay cylinder. But it is remarkable for its declarations of reform.In the ancient script, Cyrus pledges to bring relief to Babylon's citizens and return captives held prisoner in Babylon to their homelands:

▲ *Cyrus the Great.*

"I returned to the sacred cities . . . the sanctuaries of which have been in ruins for a long time, the images which used to live therein and established for them permanent sanctuaries. I gathered all their (former) inhabitants and returned (to them) their habitations."[1]

Chapter 2

THE LAND OF ANCIENT PERSIA

By 490 B.C. the Persian Empire was the largest empire that the ancient world had ever known. The Persian king, Darius I, ruled over an area that stretched east to west from the Indus River in Pakistan to Asia Minor, including Thrace, an ancient country that is now part of Bulgaria and Turkey.

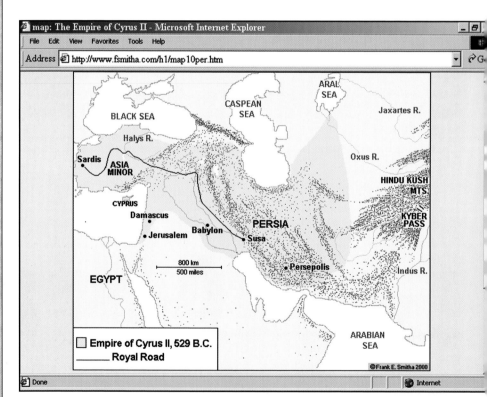

map: The Empire of Cyrus II - Microsoft Internet Explorer

File   Edit   View   Favorites   Tools   Help

Address 🗐 http://www.fsmitha.com/h1/map10per.htm

ARAL SEA

CASPEAN SEA

BLACK SEA

Jaxartes R.

Halys R.

Oxus R.

Sardis
ASIA MINOR

HINDU KUSH MTS.

CYPRUS

KYBER PASS

Damascus
Babylon
• Jerusalem

PERSIA
• Susa

800 km
500 miles

• Persepolis

Indus R.

EGYPT

☐ Empire of Cyrus II, 529 B.C.
——— Royal Road

ARABIAN SEA

©Frank E. Smitha 2000

🗐 Done

Internet

△ *The Persian Empire of Cyrus II, known as Cyrus the Great, was home to many different cultures.*

▲ *King Darius I followed by attendants. Darius expanded the system of satrapies or provinces to govern his vast empire.*

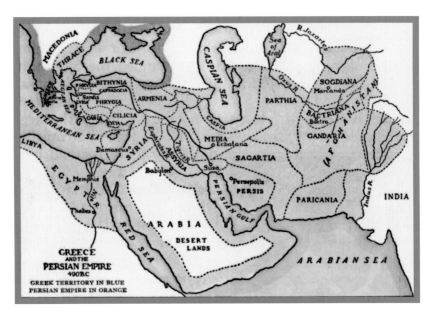

▲ Greece and Persia in 490 B.C.

The empire from north to south extended from the Caspian Sea and the Black Sea down to the Arabian Sea, the Persian Gulf, and the Red Sea. What are now parts of Pakistan, Afghanistan, Iran, Turkey, Iraq, Syria, and Egypt were all once part of the great Persian Empire.

This vast territory encompassed great desert areas, mountain ranges, seacoasts, and large fertile plains and valleys. The home area of the Persians was Persis, now called Fars, in southwestern Iran's Zagros Mountains. The wide variety of terrain included the deserts of Egypt, fertile and green only along either side of the Nile, to the mountainous terrain of Afghanistan. Large areas of the empire were desert or land so dry that crops could be grown only with large irrigation systems, which the Persians maintained throughout the empire. An inscription found in Egypt begun by Darius I and completed by Darius II describes underground channels dug for the flow of water.[1]

Chapter 3

THE HISTORY OF THE PERSIAN EMPIRE

Early reference in history to the Persians as a distinct people occurs in the records of the Assyrian Empire of the ninth to seventh centuries B.C.[1] The Assyrian records refer to the Persians and the Medes, another people in the same region. The Medes, who occupied a territory to the north of the Persians, were united and strong enough to defeat, with the aid of the Babylonians, the Assyrian Empire in 608 B.C.[2]

The Persians had formed a small kingdom in the region of modern-day Fars in Iran. The kingdom's first king, Teispes, is described on the Cyrus Cylinder as king and ancestor of Cyrus the Great.[3] However, according to an inscription ordered by Darius I, the founder of the Achaemenid dynasty was Achaemenes, father of Teispes.[4]

▶ Cyrus the Great

Cyrus II, known as "Cyrus the Great," began the Persian Empire with the conquest of the Medes' homeland, Media, in 550 B.C. Within thirty years, Cyrus had completed Persia's conquest of all the countries that would make up the Persian Empire with the exception of Egypt. Cyrus' conquest of the Medes brought Persia to the borders of Lydia on the west coast of Asia Minor. Croesus, reputed to be the richest man in the world, was Lydia's king.

Croesus invaded Persia and was defeated by Cyrus in the Lydian capital of Sardis. In 546 B.C., Croesus was taken captive, and Lydia became part of the Persian

Empire.[5] Persia's conquest of Lydia was significant since it brought under Persian domination the Ionian cities previously controlled by Lydia. The Greek city-states of Athens and Eretria then came to the aid of the Ionians, which led to the Persian wars against the mainland Greeks.

Persia now confronted the powerful Babylonian Empire, which stretched from the borders of Egypt to the borders of Persia at the Zagros Mountains. Babylonia's king, Nabonidus, was already under attack at home when Cyrus invaded Babylonia and took Nabonidus prisoner in 539 B.C. Cyrus freed the Jews who had been held in captivity in Babylon and helped them to establish a homeland in

The tomb of Cyrus the Great stands in Pasargadae, once a capital of the Persian Empire.

Palestine. His reign was characterized by a tolerance for the diverse people, languages, and religious beliefs that existed in the corners of his vast empire.

Death of Cyrus the Great and Succession of Cambyses

Before his death, Cyrus had extended his lands from the Aegean Sea in the west to the Indus River and what is today Pakistan in the far east. Cyrus had also established a system of satrapies, or provinces, in the empire that were administered by satraps, or governors. In 529 B.C., Cyrus died in battle in the northeast of the empire near the Jaxartes River.[6]

Following Cyrus' death, Cambyses II succeeded his father as the leader of the Persian Empire. Cyrus had named Cambyses as his successor, and prior to his death, Cyrus shared his rule with Cambyses.[7]

Cyrus' conquest of Babylonia had brought Persia to the borders of Egypt. Cambyses prepared to complete the conquest by first building a Persian Navy and taking control of Cyprus from the Egyptians.[8] In 525 B.C., Cambyses invaded Egypt and defeated the Egyptian pharaoh and his army at Memphis. With this victory, the once great Egyptian Empire became part of the Persian Empire, ruled by Cambyses.

Death of Cambyses and Succession of Darius I

Cambyses died in 522 B.C. on his way back to Persia to put down a rebellion led by a member of the Persian court. The leader of the rebellion was himself murdered by seven Persian nobles. One of those nobles, Darius I, then became king of the Persians in 522 B.C.[9]

▲ *Darius' mountainside memorial, known as the Behistun Inscription, proclaimed his rights as ruler and his successes in keeping the lands within his empire together.*

As soon as Darius became king, however, rebellions against his rule broke out throughout the empire, and Darius spent a year putting them down. Once he had established control over all of the Persian Empire, he marked that control by having a large memorial carved onto the face of a cliff in a mountain peak at Behistun. Now known as the Behistun Inscription, the memorial proclaimed Darius' right to the throne and his success in putting down the rebellions. The inscriptions are inscribed in Elamite, Akkadian, and the new Old Persian script that Darius ordered created especially for the memorial. The inscriptions were copied into local languages and sent throughout the empire.[10]

The Persian Wars Against the Greeks

Darius then completed a conquest of northwestern India, extending the Persian Empire east. He set about to establish a foothold in Europe by crossing the Dardanelles, a narrow strait that separates Asia Minor from Europe and connects the Aegean Sea with the Sea of Marmara. Darius' armies conquered Thrace, an ancient country on the Balkan Peninsula that had been ruled by Greece. He also formed an alliance with the king of Macedonia, an ancient kingdom north of Greece.

The stage was now set for Darius to attack the Greek mainland in the first of what would become known as the Persian Wars. In 490 B.C., a larger Persian force attacked a smaller Athenian army at Marathon, north of Athens, but was defeated. The Persians lost 6,400 men to the Athenians' 192.[11] Darius retreated back to Persia, still in control of Thrace and the Ionian cities.

Darius died in 486 B.C., having expanded the Persian Empire into southeastern Europe and what is now southern Pakistan. He proved himself the true successor to Cyrus the Great by continuing to restore the Jewish state and seeing that the Temple was rebuilt in Jerusalem in 515. Darius also expanded upon Cyrus' system of satrapies and developed a system of taxation. The great palaces at Persepolis and Susa, which were two of his capitals, were built during his reign. Finally, Darius established the absolute power of the Persian monarch, known as the King of Kings.

▶ **Xerxes' Revenge and Defeats**

Upon Darius' death in 486 B.C., he was succeeded by his son, Xerxes, who began his reign by putting down rebellions in Egypt and Babylonia. Xerxes then set about avenging his father's defeat at Marathon by launching an attack on the Greek mainland. Xerxes' aim was not only to avenge the defeat at Marathon but also to establish Persian control over the Aegean Sea and the eastern Mediterranean Sea.

In 481, Xerxes assembled an army estimated at two hundred thousand men from all over the Persian Empire.[12] It was supported by a naval fleet of one thousand ships, and both gathered at the Dardanelles to cross from Asia Minor into Europe. The powerful Greek city-states of Athens and Sparta, longtime rivals, combined

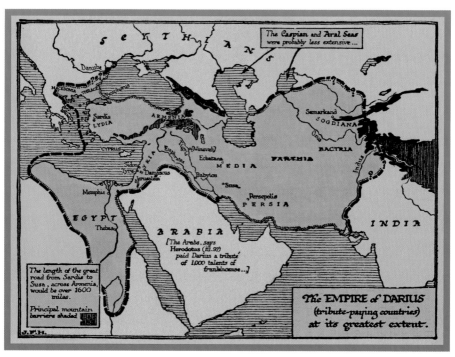

▲ At its peak, Darius' empire stretched over three continents.

their forces to fight the Persian invasion. At Thermopylae, a narrow mountain pass that led to central Greece, the Persians forced the Greeks to retreat, although a small Spartan force led by the Spartan king, Leonidas, fought bravely and delayed the Persian advance. The Persian Army then moved into Athens, which offered no resistance since its citizens had evacuated to nearby islands, and the Persians burned the city.

But after Xerxes' naval forces were defeated by the Greeks at Salamis and Plataea, Persia made no more attempts to invade mainland Greece. Instead, Persia tried to weaken the Greek city-states by bribing their leaders and assisting individual Greek states in their wars against each other. Xerxes' reign came to an end in 465 B.C. when he and his heir were murdered.

Later Achaemenid Rulers

Artaxerxes I, who next ruled Persia, may have been involved in the murder.[13]

Artaxerxes I was succeeded briefly by Xerxes II and then in 423 B.C. by his son, who took the name Darius II. After becoming king, Darius II waged war for several months against two of his brothers who tried to overthrow him. Throughout his reign, Darius II was engaged in putting down rebellions. In 404 B.C., Darius sent aid to the Spartans to assist them in their war against Athens.[14]

Darius II was succeeded by his son, Artaxerxes II, in 404 B.C. Artaxerxes II then had to battle his younger brother, Cyrus, who claimed the throne. Cyrus and the ten thousand Greek soldiers he paid to fight for him were finally defeated in battle by Artaxerxes II in 401 B.C. Artaxerxes II's reign was notable in reestablishing Persian rule over Egypt in 387 B.C., and he again put the Ionian cities under Persian control.

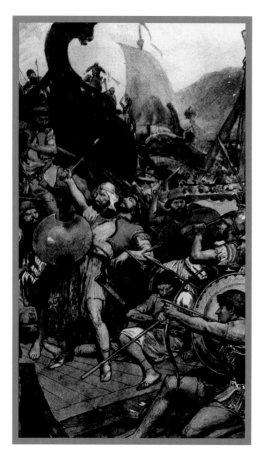

It was also the longest reign, forty-six years, of any Persian king. He died in 359 B.C.

For the next twenty-three years, the Persian Empire was again plunged into rebellion, with rightful heirs to the throne being murdered. In 336, a member of another branch of the Achaemenid family was made the ruler of Persia. Named Codomannus at birth, he took the name Darius III. Darius III would be the last Achaemenid king of the Persian Empire.

The Rise of the Hellenic League

After Philip, king of Macedonia, had established Macedonia's domination over all of the city-states of mainland Greece, he called for an invasion of the Persian Empire. He forced the formation of the Greek city-states into the Hellenic League (*Hellas* being the Greek name for "Greece") by proclaiming himself and his descendants its leader. The Hellenic League, with Philip in charge, then approved the invasion of the Persian Empire.[15]

In 336 B.C., Philip sent a force across the Dardanelles to seize a foothold in Asia Minor for the invasion of Persia. Darius III was unable to force the Greek Army back across the Dardanelles, and they remained there until Philip's son, Alexander, began his invasion of Persia.[16]

Alexander the Great Begins His Conquests

Philip was murdered in 336 B.C., and his son, Alexander, who would become known as "Alexander the Great " for his military victories, succeeded to the throne of Macedonia. Alexander had to first put down rebellions by the Greek city-states, but after that had been done, in 335 B.C., he

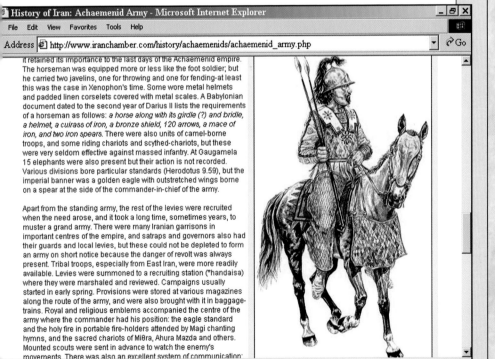

History of Iran: Achaemenid Army - Microsoft Internet Explorer

File   Edit   View   Favorites   Tools   Help

Address http://www.iranchamber.com/history/achaemenids/achaemenid_army.php   Go

it retained its importance to the last days of the Achaemenid empire. The horseman was equipped more or less like the foot soldier; but he carried two javelins, one for throwing and one for fending-at least this was the case in Xenophon's time. Some wore metal helmets and padded linen corselets covered with metal scales. A Babylonian document dated to the second year of Darius II lists the requirements of a horseman as follows: *a horse along with its girdle (?) and bridle, a helmet, a cuirass of iron, a bronze shield, 120 arrows, a mace of iron, and two iron spears*. There were also units of camel-borne troops, and some riding chariots and scythed-chariots, but these were very seldom effective against massed infantry. At Gaugamela 15 elephants were also present but their action is not recorded. Various divisions bore particular standards (Herodotus 9.59), but the imperial banner was a golden eagle with outstretched wings borne on a spear at the side of the commander-in-chief of the army.

Apart from the standing army, the rest of the levies were recruited when the need arose, and it took a long time, sometimes years, to muster a grand army. There were many Iranian garrisons in important centres of the empire, and satraps and governors also had their guards and local levies, but these could not be depleted to form an army on short notice because the danger of revolt was always present. Tribal troops, especially from East Iran, were more readily available. Levies were summoned to a recruiting station ("handaisa) where they were marshaled and reviewed. Campaigns usually started in early spring. Provisions were stored at various magazines along the route of the army, and were also brought with it in baggage-trains. Royal and religious emblems accompanied the centre of the army where the commander had his position: the eagle standard and the holy fire in portable fire-holders attended by Magi chanting hymns, and the sacred chariots of Miθra, Ahura Mazda and others. Mounted scouts were sent in advance to watch the enemy's movements. There was also an excellent system of communication:

Internet

△ *This painting portrays a fully armed member of the Achaemenid cavalry. Horses were essential to the Persian Army's military might until the last days of the Achaemenid Empire.*

began his conquest of Persia. At the river Granicus in Asia Minor, Alexander met and defeated a huge Persian Army led by Darius III's son-in-law, Mithridates, who was killed in the battle.[17]

Darius' Defeat at Issus

After the victory at Granicus, Alexander continued his march into Persia. Persian cities including Sardis and Ephesus were soon in his control, and he conquered Miletus, a seaport in western Asia Minor. Darius III had done little to stop Alexander's advance. Darius moved first to Susa and then to Babylon where he made the decision to lead his army against the Macedonian king.

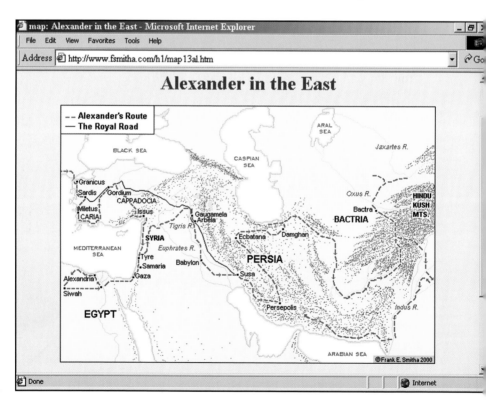

The route of Alexander's conquest.

The two armies met at Issus (which is now part of Syria) in 333 B.C. The battle was a disastrous defeat for Darius III, who fled, leaving behind the royal family and a great treasure. Darius offered Alexander ransom for the royal family as well as promising territory, but Alexander refused.[18]

Alexander's Conquest of Egypt

Alexander continued his conquests by marching down the Asia coast, conquering and subduing the Persian possessions there, including a seven-month siege at Tyre. Finally he reached Egypt and conquered it in 332 B.C.[19]

Gaugamela: Destruction of the Persian Army

In 331 B.C., Alexander marched his troops to Gaugamela, near the Tigris River in what is today Syria. There he met the Persian Army led by Darius. Alexander's forces destroyed Darius' Persian Army and Darius fled, leaving the royal treasure behind in the Persian capitals.[20] Babylon and Susa surrendered to Alexander, who marched on to Persepolis, a magnificent Persian capital whose palaces had been built by Darius I. Alexander looted and burned the city to the ground in revenge for Xerxes' destruction of the temples at Athens.[21]

End of the Achaemenid Empire: Death of Darius

Alexander continued his pursuit of Darius into the northeastern parts of the Persian Empire, but one of Darius' generals, Bessos, stabbed Darius to death in 330 B.C., as Alexander was about to catch up with them.[22] Alexander then pursued Bessos, who had declared himself king of Persia, caught him, and took him prisoner. Bessos was

Alexander of Macedon kneeling beside the body of Darius III. The death of Darius III also marked the end of the Persian Empire under the Achaemenid dynasty.

tortured, then executed in 329 B.C. as the assassin of Darius III.[23]

With the death of Darius III, the Persian Empire under the Achaemenid dynasty came to an end. Alexander would rule the Persians until his empire ended with his death in 323 in Babylon. Alexander's generals carved up his empire into several kingdoms, with Ptolemy I taking Egypt. Ptolemy's dynasty ruled Egypt until it became part of the Roman Empire in 30 B.C.

Later Persian Empires

Seleucus, who had been one of Alexander's generals, began a dynasty known as the Seleucid dynasty more than ten years after Alexander's death. The Seleucids ruled Persia and nearby regions and were responsible for founding many cities and introducing Greek culture into parts of western and central Asia. In about 250 B.C., a group known as the Parthians took control of Persia and created an empire that lasted until about A.D. 224. Their rulers were engaged in fighting Rome in the west and the Kushans in the east, in what is now Afghanistan, as well as

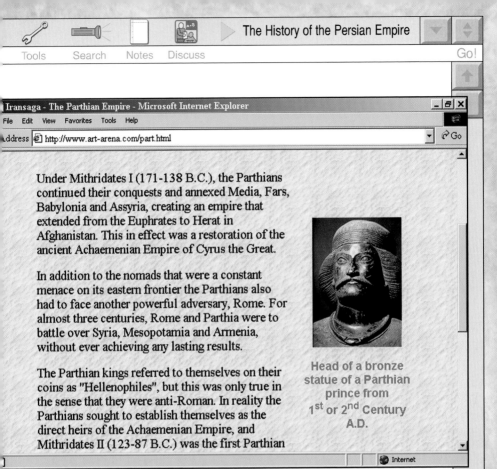

Tools   Search   Notes   Discuss   Go!

Iransaga - The Parthian Empire - Microsoft Internet Explorer

File   Edit   View   Favorites   Tools   Help

Address 🔗 http://www.art-arena.com/part.html

Under Mithridates I (171-138 B.C.), the Parthians continued their conquests and annexed Media, Fars, Babylonia and Assyria, creating an empire that extended from the Euphrates to Herat in Afghanistan. This in effect was a restoration of the ancient Achaemenian Empire of Cyrus the Great.

In addition to the nomads that were a constant menace on its eastern frontier the Parthians also had to face another powerful adversary, Rome. For almost three centuries, Rome and Parthia were to battle over Syria, Mesopotamia and Armenia, without ever achieving any lasting results.

The Parthian kings referred to themselves on their coins as "Hellenophiles", but this was only true in the sense that they were anti-Roman. In reality the Parthians sought to establish themselves as the direct heirs of the Achaemenian Empire, and Mithridates II (123-87 B.C.) was the first Parthian

Head of a bronze statue of a Parthian prince from 1st or 2nd Century A.D.

Internet

△ A bronze head of a Parthian prince.

putting down civil wars within their empire. In 224, what was left of the Persian Empire was once again controlled by a Persian, Ardashir, who overthrew the Parthians and established the Sassanid dynasty, named for Ardashir's grandfather, Sassan. The Persians continued their wars with Rome, scoring several significant victories in the mid-500s and recapturing lands that had once belonged to Persia during the Achaemenid Empire. But defeats at Constantinople, then the capital of the Byzantine Empire, made them withdraw from the lands they had conquered. With the rise of Islam in the 600s, a new religion begun in Arabia, the Sassanid dynasty came to an end.

Chapter 4

LANGUAGE AND RELIGION

The Persian kings were tolerant of the individual cultures of the countries they had conquered: They allowed the customs and languages of the conquered peoples, including those of the Egyptians, Greeks, and Babylonians, to continue.

The Persians spoke an Indo-European language known as Old Persian, which was the official language of the empire. But Aramaic, a Semitic language related to Hebrew that had long been in use in the various countries conquered by the Persians, was the most widely used language in the Persian Empire. There is no Old Persian script that has been found to exist until after the conquests. In addition to Greek writers such as Herodotus and Xenophon, Babylonian sources, and the Old Testament, a major source of our knowledge of Persia comes from royal inscriptions and official archives of the empire. Particularly important are inscriptions carved on giant memorials that offer detailed accounts of the conquests of the kings. At times the inscriptions on the monuments are carved in three languages: Elamite, the language of the earliest people in Persia; Akkadian, the language of the Babylonians; and Persian.

▶ Respect for Religious Beliefs

The Persian kings' attitude toward religion was also marked by respect and even active support of the religions of each conquered country.[1] The cuneiform inscriptions on the Cyrus Cylinder record how Cyrus the Great restored

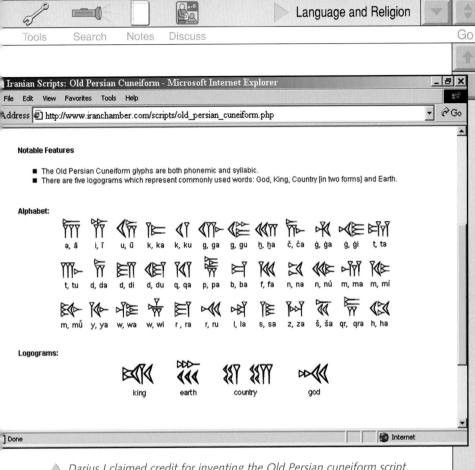

Iranian Scripts: Old Persian Cuneiform - Microsoft Internet Explorer

File   Edit   View   Favorites   Tools   Help

Address http://www.iranchamber.com/scripts/old_persian_cuneiform.php   Go

Notable Features

- The Old Persian Cuneiform glyphs are both phonemic and syllabic.
- There are five logograms which represent commonly used words: God, King, Country [in two forms] and Earth.

Alphabet:

a, ā   i, ī   u, ū   k, ka   k, ku   g, ga   g, gu   ḫ, ḫa   č, ča   ġ, ġa   ġ, ġi   t, ta

t, tu   d, da   d, di   d, du   q, qa   p, pa   b, ba   f, fa   n, na   n, nú   m, ma   m, mí

m, mū   y, ya   w, wa   w, wi   r, ra   r, ru   l, la   s, sa   z, za   š, ša   qr, qra   h, ha

Logograms:

king   earth   country   god

Done   Internet

Darius I claimed credit for inventing the Old Persian cuneiform script, whose alphabet is pictured, but most scholars think that Darius commissioned his scribes to come up with this early form of writing.

the ruined sanctuaries in Babylonia after his conquest of Babylon. Perhaps the most famous indication of the Persian kings' respect for religion comes from a passage in the Old Testament of the Christian Bible, which praises Cyrus the Great for permitting the Jews who had been exiled to Babylon to return to Jerusalem with instructions to rebuild their temple.[2] An inscription in Egypt records that Cyrus' son, Cambyses, restored Egyptian temples and worshiped in accordance with the Egyptian rites after his conquest of Egypt.[3]

According to the great teacher Zoroaster, the world is a stage for unceasing conflict between the powers of Light and Darkness, or Good and Evil.

Early Worship

Before the reign of Cyrus the Great, many people in Persia worshiped local gods or spirits associated with agriculture, war, and the important aspects of everyday life. Animals, ancestors, and the stars were all objects of worship. Worship was marked by animal sacrifice and the use of fire in the religious rites. There was no organized priesthood or religious doctrine, but learned men known as magi sometimes assisted in carrying out religious rites.[4]

Zoroastrianism and the Persians

Zoroaster was a prophet who founded a religion, Zoroastrianism, that had a great influence upon the Persian rulers of the Achaemenid dynasty. Zoroaster's exact lifetime is not known, but evidence suggests it was before Achaemenid rule.[5] Zoroaster adapted some of the older beliefs with new ideas and combined these into a unified theology. Zoroastrian beliefs were handed down orally throughout the Achaemenid period. A written text of Zoroastrian beliefs was compiled in the fourth century A.D.[6]

The Duality of Good vs. Evil

The doctrine of Zoroastrianism that existed in the Achaemenid period was based on Zoroaster's teachings that the universe was comprised of good and evil spirits constantly at war with one another. Zoroaster taught that Ahura Mazda headed the good spirits as the supreme god, representing good, light, and truth. Opposed to him were the evil spirits led by a god of darkness, Ahriman. The two gods struggled for control of the universe with men and women in the middle. The most significant features of Zoroastrianism were its belief in a supreme god and the idea that humans were free to choose between good and evil. It also taught that humans will be judged at their death, with good deeds rewarded and evil deeds punished.[7]

Zoroastrian Worship

Zoroastrian worship took place in temples and out of doors at altars, with fire playing an important part in purification rituals. Fire, together with water and earth, were revered as the natural manifestations of Ahura Mazda and were regarded as sacred. In early Zoroastrianism, magi assisted in the religious rites. Later Zoroastrian priests exercised a great influence over the government of the Achaemenid rulers, and for a time, Zoroastrianism became the state religion, although other religions continued to flourish.

Chapter 5

THE PEOPLE OF ANCIENT PERSIA

As long as they accepted Persian rule, the people living in the Persian Empire during the Achaemenid period, who were from many different ethnic groups, were allowed to live according to their own cultures, religion, and traditional practices.

▷ Families

Early in the Persian Empire, as with many ancient cultures, families were formed into clans, and clans were part of larger groups known as tribes. But with the growth of the empire, these large family units began to disappear.

Most Persian men had more than one wife, and large families were encouraged. The king even rewarded families with the most children.[1] Persian society was dominated by men, from the government led by the king to the husband in charge of the family. Men's dominance in Persian society is evident by the fact that no women appear in any of the surviving monumental reliefs of the kings and his court and subject peoples. Women also apparently began to wear veils during the reign of Cyrus the Great.[2]

Women, did, however, own and manage property, and they traveled to the far reaches of the empire when necessary to manage it. Tablets at Persepolis record how Artystone, wife of Darius I, traveled to her various estates, receiving provisions on the journey. Artystone had her own seal, which she used to sign receipts for provisions issued to her on her journeys through the empire.[3]

▲ *These figures created by skilled Persian craftsmen grace a wall in Persepolis. The figures wear the caftans typical of Persian dress.*

The clothing of the Persians mainly consisted of caftans, or long robes, and jewelry was an important part of their attire. While the nobility lived in palaces and stone houses, most commoners lived in mud huts.

▶ Farmers and Craftsmen

The Persian people who were not part of the ruling class were mostly farmers. In different parts of the empire, corn, grain, barley, sesame seed for oil, cotton, and flax were grown. Dates were another important crop. In fact, they were so important in Persia that at times they were used as money to pay debts. Cattle, sheep, and goats were raised throughout the empire.

Craftsmen were important to the ruling classes of the empire. The Persian kings employed large numbers of skilled craftsmen from many different regions. The great complex at Susa built by Darius I contains inscriptions that list craftsmen and materials from all over the empire that were used in Susa's construction. Timber from Lebanon, gold from Sardis, lapis lazuli and carnelian from Uzbekistan, ebony from Egypt, and ivory from India are among the materials and sources described. Men, women, and children from every part of the empire, including Ionia, Sardis, Babylon, Egypt, and India, were employed in the king's service as stone workers, copper-smiths, beer tenders, wine makers, and weavers.[4]

Education

There were no formal schools for the Persians living during the Achaemenid period, and only the sons of the nobility received tutoring. At the age of five, a son was removed from his mother's care to be taught the value of truth. Throughout Persian culture, it was considered disgraceful to lie. The sons of the common people were trained in horseback riding, hunting with bow and arrow, and the throwing of a spear, much as their nomadic ances-tors had been.[5]

ARTS AND CULTURAL CONTRIBUTIONS

The art of Persia was a product of the influences of the art of the conquered peoples who lived in the empire. Elements of Greek, Egyptian, and Assyrian art were taken by the Persian kings and mixed and reworked to produce an art that then became Persian.[1] The ruins of the capital at Pasargadae built by Cyrus the Great and at the great complexes built at Susa and Persepolis by Darius I show the influences of many cultures.

▷ Pasargadae

Cyrus the Great built his royal capital at Pasargadae with a number of palaces surrounded by lush gardens. The buildings featured huge columned halls decorated with monumental reliefs. Workmen from all over the empire (some who were prisoners of war) were employed in the construction of these palaces.[2] Pasargadae became the place where ceremonies marking the king's succession to the throne were held.

▷ Persepolis

Darius I began the construction of the palace complex at Persepolis, and it was continued by Xerxes and Artaxerxes I. Persepolis, built atop an artificial stone terrace, covered an area of about 1400 feet by 1000 feet. Twin staircases of 111 steps, each 23 feet wide, led to the terrace. Great columned halls were again featured in the buildings at

▲ *Ruins of buildings in Persepolis. Ionic columns decorated with carved spiral scrolls can be seen.*

△ *This griffin, a strange creature in Greek mythology, had the head and wings of an eagle and the body of a lion. This griffin is part of the artwork at the palace at Persepolis.*

Persepolis. Huge porches lined with Ionic columns, some reaching 65 feet in height, flanked the halls.[3]

▷ Monumental Reliefs

Beginning with Cyrus the Great and continued by his successors, the Persian kings recorded the history of their reigns in giant reliefs carved in stone. The stone reliefs throughout the royal buildings and on the sides of mountains featured both carved figures and inscriptions that described the important events of the king's reign. At times, the figures of the king with his followers and

servants and, sometimes, lines of prisoners, were life-size. Many of the conquered peoples are depicted in their local dress honoring the king and bearing witness to the empire's diversity. In Darius I's inscription on his tomb, he asks the viewer to look at the reliefs showing the bearers of his throne to determine the number of countries he conquered.[4] Numerous animals including horses, camels, and zebras are also carved on the reliefs. These reliefs were the testaments of the Persian kings, intended to glorify them and the empire.

Metalwork

The other major forms of art from the Achaemenid period are works of gold and silver in the form of coins and jewelry. These coins of gold and silver bore the image of the king on bent knee with a bow and arrow.[5] They were not only valuable as money but also spread the image of the king throughout the empire.

The Persians wore gold and silver bracelets, earrings, pins, belt buckles, and belts. Persian art, whether in the form of jewelry or the reliefs that bore the images and words of the kings, was the work of artisans and artists from all over the Persian Empire, particularly the Greeks and the Egyptians. But artists from all the conquered countries contributed their artistic gifts to Persian art.[6]

THE GOVERNMENT OF ANCIENT PERSIA

Under Achaemenid rule, there was no constitution or any body of law in the Persian Empire that limited the power of the king. The only limits to the king's power came from rebellion or from his own conscience. Darius I and Xerxes employed identical inscriptions to describe how they used their power to be just and protect the weak through the power that Ahura Mazda, their god, had given them.[1]

▷ The System of Satrapies

Darius I expanded upon a system begun by Cyrus the Great and divided his huge empire into twenty satrapies, governed by satraps.[2] Persis, as the homeland of the Persians, was not named a satrapy.

The satrap, or governor, of the satrapies was always a Persian, but local rulers governed under him. As long as taxes were paid and Persian rule was accepted, each satrapy was permitted to follow local laws and traditions.[3]

The satraps carried out the civil administration of the local government such as the collection of taxes and enforcement of the peace. But in times of war, the satrap raised troops and could act as a military commander.[4]

The Persian king appointed the satraps and could remove them from power on the advice of royal clerks at the satrap's court, who functioned more or less as a secret service. The royal clerk was appointed by the king and was responsible only to the king. It was the clerk's responsibility to report to the king on the activities of the satrap.[5]

▲ *Another image of Darius is captured in this stone relief carving that still stands at Persepolis, the crowning jewel of the Persian Empire.*

Tools   Search   Notes   Discuss   Go!

Communication

The vast empire was held together by a 1,500-mile highway constructed and maintained by the royal government.[6] Officials guided travelers on the roads as well as reporting on what the traveler was doing. Express riders and runners used the road to bring messages to and from the various regions of the empire. At intervals along the road were inns and fortresses with fresh supplies of men and horses.[7] In this, the Persian Empire was the first to have a postal system, which functioned much like the Pony Express system of the nineteenth-century United States. Communication from the satrapies to the royal government was assisted by the use of messages flashed by fire and mirrors.

The Kings' Revenue

The Persian kings acquired a great deal of their wealth through conquest, but the kings' revenue was also supplemented by taxes. Generally, each satrapy paid a fixed amount of taxes in silver.[8] In addition, some taxes were paid through the taxation of local products and were used to feed government workers and troops.[9] Darius I imposed a tax on goods moved through canals in Babylonia.

Gifts were another important source of the Persian kings' wealth. The gifts could be precious materials such as gold and silver, but they also included presents of cattle, sheep, fruit, and wine. As the king and his court made regular travels throughout the empire, they were fed and housed by the local people, who considered this their gift to the king. Such gifts could amount to a huge expense, however, as the king traveled with an extremely large number of people, excluding portions of his army.

The Achaemenid kings produced for the first time in history a vast empire of widely differing cultures that were

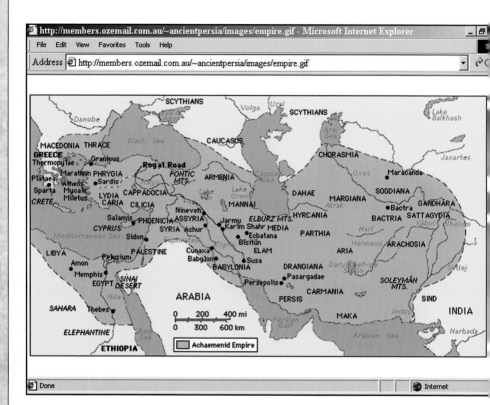

▲ *The greatest extent of the Achaemenid Empire.*

united under one ruler. The Persian Empire, under Achaemenid rule, gave birth to the idea of multiculturalism: a vast number of people from different backgrounds, living together in peace, with secure borders, under one ruler, and free to trade and exchange ideas and cultures with one another.[10]

Chapter Notes

Chapter 1. The Empire of Cyrus the Great

1. Inscription, the Cyrus Cylinder, Yale University Library, "Ancient Seals From the Babylonian Collection," n.d., <http://www.library.yale.edu/judaica/exhibits/webarch/front/BabylonianCollection.html#cylinderone> (February 2, 2004).

Chapter 2. The Land of Ancient Persia

1. J.M. Cook, *The Persians* (London: The Orion Publishing Group Ltd., 1989), p. 106.

Chapter 3. The History of the Persian Empire

1. Amélie Kuhrt, *The Ancient Near East, Volume Two* (London-New York: Routledge, 1998), p. 652.

2. Ibid., p. 545.

3. Josef Wiesehöfer, translated by Azizeh Azodi, *Ancient Persia from 550 B.C. to 650 A.D.* (London-New York: I.B. Tauris & Co., Ltd., 2001), pp. 44–45.

4. J.M. Cook, *The Persians* (London: The Orion Publishing Group Ltd., 1989), pp. 10–11.

5. Kuhrt, p. 658.

6. Cook, p. 54.

7. Ibid., p. 55.

8. Kuhrt, p. 662.

9. Ibid., p. 664.

10. Cook, p. 100.

11. Michael Grant, *The Classical Greeks* (United States: Book-of-the-Month Club, Inc., 1997), p. 6.

12. John Haywood, with Charles Freeman, Paul Garwood, and Judith Toms, *Historical Atlas of the Classical World 500 B.C.–A.D. 600* (Cordoba, Spain: Barnes & Noble Books, 2002), p. 207.

13. Kuhrt, p. 671.

14. Ibid., p. 673.

15. Peter Green, *Alexander of Macedon, 356–323 B.C.* (Berkeley and Los Angeles: University of California Press, 1991), p. 94.

16. Cook, p. 338.

17. Green, pp. 179–180.

18. Cook, p. 341.

19. Chester G. Starr, *A History of the Ancient World* (New York: Oxford University Press, 1991), p. 398.

20. Cook, p. 342.

21. Green, pp. 319–320.

22. Cook, p. 343.

23. Green, p. 355.

Chapter 4. Language and Religion

1. Josef Wiesehöfer, translated by Azizeh Azodi, *Ancient Persia from 550 B.C. to 650 A.D.* (London-New York: I.B. Tauris & Co., Ltd., 2001), p. 57.

2. Ibid., p. 44.

3. Amélie Kuhrt, *The Ancient Near East, Volume Two* (London-New York: Routledge, 1998), p. 663.

4. J.M. Cook, *The Persians* (London: The Orion Publishing Group Ltd., 1989), p. 228.

5. Ibid., p. 232.

6. Wiesehöfer, p. 95.

7. Sandra Mackey, *The Iranians, Persia, Islam and the Soul of a Nation* (New York: The Penguin Group, 1996), pp. 16–17.

Chapter 5. The People of Ancient Persia

1. Josef Wiesehöfer, translated by Azizeh Azodi, *Ancient Persia from 550 B.C. to 650 A.D.* (London-New York: I.B. Tauris & Co., Ltd., 2001), p. 36.

2. Sandra Mackey, *The Iranians, Persia, Islam and the Soul of a Nation* (New York: The Penguin Group, 1996), pp. 16–17.

3. Wiesehöfer, p. 69.

4. Cook, pp. 129–130.

5. Amélie Kuhrt, *The Ancient Near East, Volume Two* (London-New York: Routledge, 1998), p. 683.

Chapter 6. Arts and Cultural Contributions

1. Sandra Mackey, *The Iranians, Persia, Islam and the Soul of a Nation* (New York: The Penguin Group, 1996), p. 29.

2. Amélie Kuhrt, *The Ancient Near East, Volume Two* (London-New York: Routledge, 1998), p. 661.

3. J.M. Cook, *The Persians* (London: The Orion Publishing Group Ltd., 1989), pp. 236–238.

4. Kuhrt, p. 677.

5. Cook, p. 103.

6. Ibid., p. 247.

Chapter 7. The Government of Ancient Persia

1. Amélie Kuhrt, *The Ancient Near East, Volume Two* (London-New York: Routledge, 1998), p. 689.

2. J.M. Cook, *The Persians* (London: The Orion Publishing Group Ltd., 1989), p. 116.

3. Kuhrt, pp. 689–690.

4. Cook, p. 126.

5. Ibid., p. 126.

6. Richard F. Nyrop, ed., *Iran: A Country Study* (Washington, D.C.: The American University, 1978), p. 25.

7. Josef Wiesehöfer, translated by Azizeh Azodi, *Ancient Persia from 550 B.C. to 650 A.D.* (London-New York: I.B. Tauris & Co., Ltd., 2001), p. 77.

8. Cook, p. 303.

9. Wiesehöfer, p. 67.

10. Cook, p. 344.

Brown, Alan, and Andrew Langley. *What I Believe.* Brookfield, Conn.: Millbrook Press, 1999.

Cartlidge, Cherese, and Charles Clark. *Iran.* Farmington Hills, Mich.: Gale Group, 2002.

Cheshire, Gerard, and Paula Hammond. *The Middle East.* Broomall, Pa.: Mason Crest Publishers, 2003.

Chrisp, Peter. *Alexander the Great: Legend of a Warrior King.* New York: Dorling Kindersley, 2000.

Coote, Roger. *Ancient Civilizations.* New York: Smithmark, 1992.

Crompton, Samuel Willard. *Alexander the Great.* Philadelphia: Chelsea House Publishers, 2003.

Habeeb, William Mark. *Iran.* Philadephia: Mason Crest Publishers, 2003.

Nardo, Don. *Life in Ancient Persia.* San Diego, Calif.: Blackbirch Press, 2004.

Spencer, Lauren. *Iran: A Primary Source Cultural Guide.* New York: Rosen Publishing Group, 2003.

The Visual Dictionary of Ancient Civilizations. New York: Dorling Kindersley, 1994.

Wagner, Heather Lehr. *Iran.* Broomall, Pa.: Chelsea House Publishers, 2002.

Index